"We work in the dark. We do what we can. We give what we have. Our doubt is our passion. Our passion is our task. The rest is the madness of art."

Henry James

Books by Denise Levertov

Poetry

Collected Earlier Poems 1940-1960

The Jacob's Ladder

O Taste and See

The Sorrow Dance

Relearning the Alphabet

To Stay Alive

Footprints

The Freeing of the Dust

Life in the Forest

Prose

The Poet in the World

Translations

Guillevic/Selected Poems

Denise Levertov

Life
in
the
Forest

A New Directions Book

ACKNOWLEDGMENTS
Grateful acknowledgment is made to the editors of magazines and books in which some of the poems in this volume first appeared: *American Poetry Review, Anglican Theological Review, Atropos* (Quebec), *Beloit Poetry Journal, Boston University Journal, Boundary 2, College of Wooster Yearbook, Dartmouth Medical School Journal, The Hampden-Sydney Poetry Review, Hanging Loose, Harper's Magazine, In Our Own Words, Liberation, Mad Dog* (Wales), *Moons and Lion Tailes, Mother Jones, New Letters, Pearl* (Denmark), *The Poetry Miscellany, San Marcos Review, WIP, Ontario Review,* and *Wild Places.*

'Chekhov on the West Heath' was first published in a limited edition by Woolmer & Brotherston, Ltd., Gladstone Hollow, Andes, New York. The section 'Modulations for Solo Voice' also first appeared as a limited edition, brought out by Five Trees Press, 660 York Street, San Francisco, California.

Manufactured in the United States of America
First published clothbound and as
New Directions Paperbook 461 in 1978
Published simultaneously in Canada by George J. McLeod Ltd., Toronto.

Library of Congress Cataloging in Publication Data
Levertov, Denise, 1923–
    Life in the forest.
    (A New Directions Book)
    I. Title.
PS3562.E8876L5   811'5'4   78–9356
ISBN 0–8112–0692–0
ISBN 0–8112–0693–9 pbk.

New Directions Books are published for James Laughlin
by New Directions Publishing Corporation,
80 Eighth Avenue, New York 10011

SECOND PRINTING

Contents

In 1975 or '6 I found in Cesare Pavese's poems of the
1930's, *Lavorare Stanca*, read in the Penguin edition trans-
lated by Margaret Crosland, a kind of ratification for a
direction I was already obscurely taking in my own work.
Pavese's beautiful poems are about various persons other
than himself; though he is a presence in them also, their
focus is definitely not autobiographical and egocentric,
and in his accompanying essays he speaks of his concept
of suggesting a narrative through the depiction of a scene,
a landscape, rather than through direct recounting of
events as such. The poems I had been moving towards
were impelled by two forces: first, a recurring need—dealt
with earlier by resort to a diarylike form, a poem long
enough to include prose passages and discrete lyrics—to
vary a habitual lyric mode; not to abandon it, by any
means, but from time to time to explore more expansive
means; and second, the decision to try to avoid overuse of
the autobiographical, the dominant first-person singular of
so much of the American poetry—good and bad—of recent
years.

Those poems of my own which have, I feel, some humble
affinity—however oblique—with what Pavese achieved in
Lavorare Stanca, tend to rather long lines and a discursive
structure. The content of the last five of them is, however,
shared by certain other poems—the first three of *Con-
tinuum*—that do not belong, in tone and structure, to the
Homage to Pavese section of this book. This is not wholly
true of 'A Soul-Cake': formally it could belong with the
Homage to Pavese poems; but its more emphatic use of the
first person unfits it for that group. By placing it, together
with 'A Visit' and 'Death Psalm,' at the beginning of *Con-
tinuum*, I hope to suggest to the reader alternative ways
of reading all eight poems—i.e., they can be considered as
belonging to their respective sections, or they can be read
as an internal grouping that spans the two sections.

vii

The poem in *Homage to Pavese* called 'Chekhov on the West Heath' grew out of being asked to contribute something to the Chekhov Festival organized by James McConkey at Cornell University early in 1977. Though originally I had considered presenting a prose piece I found myself stimulated into a poem. In this instance I felt that, despite the frankly autobiographical standpoint taken, the poem belonged in the 'Pavese' section by virtue of its focus on other persons and on place.

The group called *Modulations for Solo Voice* appeared in a limited edition published by Five Trees Press in San Francisco as a benefit to provide funds for publication of a young, unknown, woman poet. These poems are definitely a sequence, and make the most sense read in the order in which they are arranged—which, however, differs from that of their original printing in one particular: the last two poems are reversed, what was originally called 'Litany' now becoming the coda or 'Epilogue.'

Throughout the rest of the book the arrangement is less chronological than by kind and, within such kinship groups, by internal association from poem to poem.

HOMAGE TO PAVESE

Human being—walking
in doubt from childhood on: walking

a ledge of slippery stone in the world's woods
deep-layered with wet leaves—rich or sad: on one
side of the path, ecstasy, on the other
dull grief.   Walking

the mind's imperial cities, roofed-over alleys,
                                thoroughfares, wide boulevards
that hold evening primrose of sky in steady calipers.

Always the mind
walking, working, stopping sometimes to kneel
in awe of beauty, sometimes leaping, filled with the energy
of delight, but never able to pass
the wall, the wall
of brick that crumbles and is replaced,
of twisted iron,
of rock,
the wall that speaks, saying monotonously:

        Children and animals
                        who cannot learn
        anything from suffering,
        suffer, are tortured, die
        in incomprehension.

This human being, each night nevertheless
summoning—with a breath blown at a flame,
                                or hand's touch
on the lamp-switch—darkness,
                        silently utters,
impelled as if by a need to cup the palms

3

and drink from a river,
                    the words, 'Thanks.
Thanks for this day, a day of my life.'
                              And wonders.
Pulls up the blankets, looking
into nowhere, always in doubt.
And takes strange pleasure
in having repeated once more the childish formula,
a pleasure in what is seemly.
And drifts to sleep, downstream
on murmuring currents of doubt and praise,
the wall shadowy, that tomorrow
will cast its own familiar, chill, clear-cut shadow
into the day's brilliance.

. . . after three years—a 3-decker novel
in fifteen pages? Which beginning
to begin with? 'Since I saw you last,
the doctor has prescribed me artificial tears,
a renewable order . . .' But that leaves out
the real ones. Shall I write about them?
What about comedy, laughter, good news?
'I live in a different house now,
but can give you news
of most of the same people . . .' That ignores
the significance of the house, its tone of voice,
and the sentence by sentence
unfolding of lives into chapters.
'Your last letter told about sand-dunes in winter,
and having the sea to yourself.
Beautiful; I read it to the strangers
in whose midst I was at the time.
And that's the way we lost touch for so long,
my response was the reading aloud
instead of a letter,
and we both moved house—
a shifting of sand underfoot . . .'

Well, I could echo
the sound of facts, their weather—
thunderclaps, rain hitting stone, rattle of windows.
And spaces would represent sunlight,
when the wind gave over and everyone rested
between the storms.
Or chronological narrative? 'In the spring
of '73,' . . . 'That summer,'
'By then it was fall . . .'
                        All or nothing—
and that would be nothing,
dust, parchment dried up, invisible ink.

5

Maybe I'll leave the whole story
for you to imagine,
telling you only, 'A year ago,
I said farewell to that poplar you will remember,
that gave us its open secret,
pressed on us all we could grasp, and more,
of vibrating, silvergreen being,
a tree tripping over its phrases in haste,
eloquent aspen.'

I know you know
it took my farewell for granted:
what it had given, it would never take back.
I know you know
about partings, tears, eyedrops, revisions, dwellings,
                                                    discoveries,
mine or yours; those are the glosses,
Talmudic tractates, a lifetime's study. The Word itself
is what we heard, and shall always hear, each leaf
imprinted, syllables in our lives.

Tough guy. Star of David
and something in Hebrew—a motto—
hang where Catholics used to dangle
St. Christopher (now discredited).
No smile. White hair. American-born,
I'd say, maybe the Bronx.
When another cab pulls alongside
at a light near the Midtown Tunnel, and its driver
rolls down his window and greets this guy
with a big happy face and a first-name greeting,
he bows like a king, a formal acknowledgement,
and to me remarks,
                    deadpan,
            'Seems to think he knows me.'

'You mean you don't know him?'—I lean forward laughing,
close to the money-window.
                        'Never seen him before in my life.'
Something like spun steel floats invisible, until
                              questions strike it,
all round him, the way light gleams webs among
                              grass in fall.
And on we skim
in silence past the cemeteries, into
the airport, ahead of time. He's beat
the afternoon traffic. I tip him well.
A cool acceptance. Cool? It's
cold as ice.

        Yet I've seen,
squinting to read his license,
how he smiled—timidly?—anyway,
smiled, as if hoping to please,
at the camera. My heart

stabs me. Somewhere this elderly
close-mouthed skeptic hides
longing and hope. Wanted
—immortalized for the cops, for his fares, for the world—
to be looking his best.

Nightingale Road

How gold their hair was,
and how their harps
and sweet voices called out into the valley
summer nights!

The boys black-haired,
coming home black with coal dust, same as us all,
but milk-skinned when they'd had their wash.
One of the boys, Arthur,
went down the pit the first time
same day as me.

And the girls—that gold hair
twining like pea-vine tendrils,
and even the youngest could play her harp.

Up on the mountain their house was,
up Nightingale Street, and then as you leave the village
it's Nightingale Road.
Mother and father, the three boys
and the six girls; all of them singing,
you'd think the gates of Heaven were open.

And funny thing—
the T.B. didn't stop them
each one, till a few weeks only
before it took them.
One by one
the whole family went, though.

Oh, but the sound was fine!
I'd be a young boy, lying awake,
and I'd smell my Mam's
honeysuckle she'd got growing
up the house wall, and I'd hear them singing,
a regular choir they were,
and the harps rippling out

and somehow as I'd be falling asleep
I couldn't tell which was the music
and which was that golden hair they had,
and all with that milky skin. The voices
sweet and gold and shrill and the harps
flowing like milk.

S. *Wales*, circa *1890*

for Jim McConkey
who spurred me into writing it
and for Rebecca Garnett
who was and is 'Bet'

A young girl in a wheelchair, •
another girl pushing the chair.
Up from Heath Mansions they go,
past the long brick wall of the Fenton House garden.
The invalid girl's hands move as she speaks, delicately,
describing the curve of a cloud.
The other, younger one comes into focus;
how could I know so well
the back of my own head? I could touch the hair
of the long plait . . . Ah,
that's it: the young girl painting
in Corot's *L'Atelier,* upright, absorbed,
whose face we don't see. *There I am,*
I thought, the first time I saw it,
startled.
Up through small streets they go,
the crest of the hill, a stonesthrow of unpaved lane,
and out to the terrace: a few
lopsided benches, tussocky grass,
and the great billowing prospect north.
This is Hampstead. This
is Judge's Walk. It is nineteen hundred
and forty-one.
The war? They take it for granted;
it was predicted while they were children,
and has come to pass. It means
no more ballet school, Betty is ill,
I am beginning to paint in oils.
The war is simply
how the world is, to which they were born.
They share

10

the epiphanies of their solitudes,
hardly knowing or speaking to anyone else
their own age. They have not discovered men
or sex at all. But daily
they live! Live
intensely. Mysterious fragrance
gentles the air
under the black poplars.
And Bet, looking off towards hawthorn and willow,
middle-distance of valley and steep small hills,
says she would like to bounce
from one round-topped tree to another,
in the spring haze.

Often and often, as they talk and gaze,
that year and the next,
                        Chekhov is with them.
With us.
        The small, dark-green volumes.
        The awkward, heroic versions.
We're not systematic,
we don't even *try* to read all of them, held secure
in conviction of endless largesse.

                            Bet's glinting hair
in tendrils around her face. Her hands
thin. A spirit
woven of silk, has grown in her, as if bodily strength,
dwindling, had been a cocoon,
                        and only by this strange weakness
could her intelligence be freed, that instructs
the poet in me.
Alone at home, in between visits, I write, paint,
read and read, practice *Für Elise* with feeling
                            (and too much pedal)
help with the housework or shirk it,
and wait.

11

What did he say to us, Chekhov? Who was this Chekhov
pacing the round of the Whitestone Pond,
his hand on the chair coming down Heath Street,
telling the tale of Kashtanka in the gloomy sickroom
back at Heath Mansions?
                                        Ah, even though
the dark gauze of youth
swaddled us,
                        while airraids and news of battle
were part of each ominous day, and in flashes of dread
we glimpsed invasion, England and Europe gone down
utterly into the nightmare;
                                        even though Bet
was fading, month by month, and no one knew why—
we were open to life and hope: it was that he gave us,
generous, precise, lifting us
into the veins of a green leaf, translucent,
setting our hearts' tinder alight,
                                        sun striking on glass to release
the latent flames.

When the Black Monk
swiftly drew near, a whirlwind column grown
                                        from a pinpoint
to giant size, then—shrinking to human measure,
and passing inaudibly—moved through the solid trees
to vanish like smoke,
                                        we thrilled to the presence of a power,
unquestioning. We knew
everything and nothing, nothing and everything.
Glimpsing a verity we could not define,
we saw that the story is not about illusion,
it's about what is true: 'the great garden
        with its miraculous flowers,
        the pines with their shaggy roots,
        the ryefield, marvellous science, youth,
        daring, joy . . .' That was the Chekhov we knew.

12

And the betrothed girl, who listens and listens
to a different and useful life calling her, and *does*
wrench herself free and go to study—and more,
comes back and *again* frees herself, journeying forth
(because a man dying, who himself
could not be free, gave her
his vision) into the hard, proto-revolutionary future,
her step forward for all of us,
as his words were for her—she was the Chekhov
who slipped unrecognized into our dreaming days.
She was at Bet's side when Bet,
a woman with grown children, so changed
from the girl in the wheelchair, a woman alone
with years of struggle behind her, sturdy—
yet still afraid—began, in spite of her fear,
to learn to teach. And at *my* side
in Berkeley, Boston, Washington, when we held our line
before advancing troopers, or sang out, 'Walk,
don't run,' retreating from gas and billyclubs,

                                 trying to learn
to act in the world.
                 She, The Betrothed,
whose marriage was not with her fiancé but with her life's
need to grow, to work for Chekhov's
     'Holy of holies—the human body, health, intelligence,
     inspiration, love,
     and the most absolute
     freedom from violence and lying'—she
was the Chekhov we knew.

                   What he would mean to us
we still can know only in part. (What has the Heath,
which Bet has lived close to always, and I,
through decades away, never quite lost sight of,
meant in our lives? A place of origin
gives and gives, as we return to it,
bringing our needs.) What he has meant
and goes on meaning, can't be trapped
into closed definition. But it has to do
not with failure, defeat, frustration,

Moscows never set out for,
but with love.
                    The sharp steel
of his scorn for meanness and cruelty gleamed
over our sheltered heads only half-noticed,
and irony was beyond our grasp,
we couldn't yet laugh with him; nevertheless
some inkling of rectitude and compassion
came to us, breathed in
under the fragrant leaves in wartime London, to endure
somewhere throughout the tumult of years. How,
                                        in our crude,
vague, dreamy ignorance could we recognize
       'the subtle, elusive beauty of human grief'?
Yet from between the dark green bindings
it rose, wafting into us, ready
to bide its time. The man who imagined a ring
inscribed with the words, 'Nothing passes,'
that rich man's son whom the townsfolk called
                                        'Small Gain,'
who suffered loss after loss, and was
                                        'left with the past,'
he too—for beyond despair
he carried in him the seed of change, the vision,
seeing not only *what is* but *what might be*—
he too was the Chekhov we knew, unknowing.

                              As we looked out
into the haze from that open height
familiar to Keats and Constable in their day—
a place built not only of earth but of layers
of human response, little hill
in time, in history—
your smile, Chekhov, 'tender, delightful, ironic,'
looked over our shoulders; and still looks, now,
half of our lifetime gone by, or more,
till we turn to see
who you were, who you are, everpresent, vivid,
luminous dust.

14

A Woman Meets an Old Lover

'He with whom I ran hand in hand
kicking the leathery leaves down Oak Hill Path
thirty years ago,

appeared before me with anxious face, pale,
almost unrecognized, hesitant,
lame.

He whom I cannot remember hearing laugh out loud
but see in mind's eye smiling, self-approving,
wept on my shoulder.

He who seemed always
to take and not give, who took me
so long to forget,

remembered everything I had so long forgotten.'

When she cannot be sure
which of two lovers it was with whom she felt
this or that moment of pleasure, of something fiery
streaking from head to heels, the way the white
flame of a cascade streaks a mountainside
seen from a car across a valley, the car
changing gear, skirting a precipice,
climbing . . .
When she can sit or walk for hours after a movie
talking earnestly and with bursts of laughter
with friends, without worrying
that it's late, dinner at midnight, her time
spent without counting the change . . .
When half her bed is covered with books
and no one is kept awake by the reading light
and she disconnects the phone, to sleep till noon . . .
Then
selfpity dries up, a joy
untainted by guilt lifts her.
She has fears, but not about loneliness;
fears about how to deal with the aging
of her body—how to deal
with photographs and the mirror. She feels
so much younger and more beautiful
than she looks. At her happiest
—or even in the midst of
some less than joyful hour, sweating
patiently through a heatwave in the city
or hearing the sparrows at daybreak, dully gray,
toneless, the sound of fatigue—
a kind of sober euphoria makes her believe
in her future as an old woman, a wanderer,
seamed and brown,
little luxuries of the middle of life all gone,
watching cities and rivers, people and mountains,

without being watched; not grim nor sad,
an old winedrinking woman, who knows
the old roads, grass-grown, and laughs to herself . . .
She knows it can't be:
that's Mrs. Doasyouwouldbedoneby from
                                    The Water-Babies,
no one can walk the world any more,
a world of fumes and decibels.
But she thinks maybe
she could get to be tough and wise, some way,
anyway. Now at least
she is past the time of mourning,
now she can say without shame or deceit,
O blessed Solitude.

He is scared of the frankness of women
which attracts and, when he draws near to listen,
may repulse or ignore him. This morning
in lazy sunlight's veil of clear and pale honey
poured from the sky's blue spoon,
they were laughing, talking over coffee about
misadventures, lovers, their own bodies,
and didn't stop when he came to join them, stepping
from indoor shade onto the charmed
and dappled stone ground of their terrace.

If any one of them had been
alone there, surely
his presence would have changed her,
he'd have seen that flicker, the putting aside
of her solitude to make room for him?
Together they seem almost blind to him.

Later, when they have gone to see bubbles of glass
blown into phantasmagoric precisions,
he takes a gondola, sliding past the palazzos,
and counts bridges. It's not (he thinks to himself
at some dark place in his mind, an intersection
of narrow seldom-navigated canals) that I want
their entire attention: that would demand—oh,
a response
nothing assures me I can give.
It's that when I see
their creature freedom, the way they can
fling themselves into the day!—as I,
being a strong swimmer, fling myself sometimes
into the ocean off a sailboat:
then I envy them.

If they had stopped (he wonders)
when I came out to their table,
interrupted themselves to acknowledge me alien,
would I have felt more excluded or less?
Their frankness, their uninterrupted friendship,
the sunlight lacing their hair, their
bright clothes, the three of them, their eyes
friendly but without mercy, without
the mercy of distance . . . When they
admit me, passing the creamjug,
to their laughter, laughter and even
   the confession of their own
troubles, about which they speak
so simply, so freely,
I am afraid.

The gondola shoots back out
as if with a sighing triumph into the breadth
and glitter of the Grand Canal,
the golden façades, vaporetti bustling,
pigeons wheeling up from the piazza.
He pays the silent gondolier, to whom
he has nothing to say, no way
to convince him he is a person,
and lands, to stroll
back to the hotel, back to wait
till the women return,
drawn by what he fears.

A handsome fullgrown child, he seems,
in his well-chosen suit and wedding-ring,
hair not too long or short, taking
a business trip, surely one of his first—

listening enthralled to the not-much-older
bearded man in the window seat,
a returned mercenary, bragging of Africa:
bronzed, blondish, imperial pirate
halfaudible, thrillingly, under the jet's monotonous
subdued growling.

The baby businessman, naïf, laughs, excitement
springing from him in little splashes—his aura
fragmented—at a whiff of
soiled romance. It is something morbid
that flutters his dark thick lashes, gestures
with such well-cared-for hands,

hands his young wife
must want to bite, when they fumble,
innocent and impatient,
at her tense thighs.

May 1976

A Mystery (Oaxaca, Mexico)

A gust of night rain lightly
sweeps the dusty *Zocalo*, and the moon is down.
Mariachis are wrapping soft old cloths
around their instruments, and laying them reverently
in dingy cases, the way peasant grandsons
wrap ancient grandmothers,

                            laying them back in their cribs.
The last tourists, watched by waiters whose features
are carved by obsidian knives to regard
bloodsacrifice, are on the move
under the *portales*, pushing back chairs,
draining a last *cerveza Moctezuma*, leaving
here a forgotten *US News*, there

                        a half-full pack of Luckies
some beer spilled on;

                and the sound of their voices,
Texans, New Englanders, hippies from California,
all the same to him, nasal and familiar, dwindles
as they scatter to sleep or sex or cards
or whatever the *yanquis* do by night.
Decades he has passed
back and forth and around and back and forth
in this square; and always the weight
of many *serapes*, heavy, and in the sun, hot,
on his shoulder. Of course he makes sales,
he spreads out the topmost one so they can see
the whole design. Some ignore him, some
wave him away, some he knows and nods to sometimes,

                            they come
year after year and no longer buy, but they once did or

                              still might—
but always there are some new ones, eager,

                       easily impressed—yes,
he sells, he is not poor—no, looking around him

                    he can see that anyone

looking from him to the shoeshine men, even,
not to speak of the barefoot boys with trays of quivering
ruby and gold and emerald *gelatinas,*
or the women nursing their babies down in the dust,
                                                ignoring
the ceaseless buzzing of wasps that are drunk all day
on candied fruits that sell by the piece,
women who take home scarcely the price of supper—
anyone looking from them to him can see he's not poor,
as poor goes. He's in business,
that's how he likes to think of himself. But still
he keeps walking, leaning always a bit
to one side from the weight.
                                        He can't remember
his boyhood well. When he was young there was
                                something he wanted badly,
some desire that flamed in his eyes once,
like a spiralling saint's-day star it was,
rising from the heart when someone, something,
put a match to it . . . What was it? He's calm, but
                                                there's something
he can't remember.

The *tejedoras,* weavers,
Trixe women from the mountains, who all day
sit at work in the *Alameda* under the trees,
have gone with their little looms, their children,
                                the two or three men
who come down from their villages with them,
                                gone for the night
to sleep wherever they sleep.
The dome of the bandstand gleams, rainsprinkled, lit
by the tall street-lamps whose light
is somehow more silent and steady than darkness.
Here and there, now, one can see a few grayish figures
that have not left for the night's rest
but have begun to take it, tucked
as best they can into the angle of wall and sidewalk

22

or, if they dare, in a doorway,
some drunk, some homeless, all, certainly
of a poverty he has no truck with. Still,
he keeps walking. The bells of two unsynchronized
clocks are ringing:—eleven—midnight. A dog's howling
down by the market somewhere. The chairs and tables
from the cafés on three sides of the *Zocalo*
have been taken in or stacked—the fourth side,
floodlit, elegant, menacing, guarded always, is The Police,
The Government—a palace.
      There's no-one
to whom to open the topmost *serape*,
outshaking its firm folds, to display
a god, a bird, a geometry some say
has some intention. No one to speak to. *'Este jardin*
es suyo. Cuidelo,' say the signs among grass and flowers;
deterrent branches of thorns have been strewn on the
          neat parterres.
          A stranger,
crossing the *Zocalo* at a distance, solitary, glances his way.
He doesn't know that the stranger thinks,
'Doesn't the old man ever long
simply to put down his weight of woven wool
and lie down? Lie down and rest?
Here, anywhere, now,
and be still? He's been carrying through the years
a nest of blankets, a bed—heavier
than I can imagine . . . If that temptation were mine,
what could keep me walking, walking,
always carrying my wares? I'd lie down
as if in the snow . . .'

The 90th Year

for Lore Segal

High in the jacaranda shines the gilded thread
of a small bird's curlicue of song—too high
for her to see or hear.
                          I've learned
not to say, these last years,
'O, look!—O, listen, Mother!'
as I used to.

            (It was she
who taught me to look;
to name the flowers when I was still close to the ground,
my face level with theirs;
or to watch the sublime metamorphoses
unfold and unfold
over the walled back gardens of our street . . .

It had not been given her
to know the flesh as good in itself,
as the flesh of a fruit is good. To her
the human body has been a husk,
a shell in which souls were prisoned.
Yet, from within it, with how much gazing
her life has paid tribute to the world's body!
How tears of pleasure
would choke her, when a perfect voice,
deep or high, clove to its note unfaltering!)

She has swept the crackling seedpods,
the litter of mauve blossoms, off the cement path,
tipped them into the rubbish bucket.
She's made her bed, washed up the breakfast dishes,
wiped the hotplate. I've taken the butter and milkjug
back to the fridge next door—but it's not my place,

24

visiting here, to usurp the tasks
that weave the day's pattern.
Now she is leaning forward in her chair,
         by the lamp lit in the daylight,
rereading *War and Peace*.
                   When I look up
from her wellworn copy of *The Divine Milieu*,
which she wants me to read, I see her hand
loose on the black stem of the magnifying glass,
she is dozing.
'I am so tired,' she has written to me, 'of appreciating
the gift of life.'

When she was in the strangers' house—
    good strangers, almost relatives, good house,
    so familiar, known for twenty years,
    its every sound at once, and without thought,
    interpreted:
                but alien, deeply alien—
when she was there last week, part of her wanted
only to leave. It said, *I must escape*—no,
crudely, in the vernacular: *I gotta get outta here,*
it said.

And part of her
ached for her mother's pain,
her dying here—at home, yet far away from home,
thousands of miles of earth and sea, and ninety years
from her roots. The daughter's one happiness
during the brief visit that might be her last
(no, last but one: of course there would always be
what had stood for years at the end of some highway of
factual knowledge, a terminal wall;
there would be words to deal with: funeral, burial,
                     disposal of effects;
the books to pack up)—her one happiness *this* time
was to water her mother's treasured, fenced-in garden,
a Welsh oasis where she remembers adobe rubble
two decades ago. Will her mother now
ever rise from bed, walk out of her room,
                     see if her yellow rose
has bloomed again?
Rainbows, the dark earthfragrance, the whisper of
                     arched spray:
the pleasure goes back
to the London garden, forty, fifty years ago,
her mother younger than *she* is now.
And back in the north, watering the blue ajuga

                    (far from beginnings too, but it's a place
                    she's chosen as home)
the daughter knows
another, hidden part of her longed—or longs—
for her mother to be her mother again,
consoling, judging, forgiving,
whose arms were once
                    strong to hold her and rock her,
who used to chant
                    a ritual song that did magic
to take away hurt. Now mother is child, helpless; her mind
is clear, her spirit proud, she can even laugh—
but half-blind, half-deaf, and struck down
in body, she's a child in being at the mercy
of looming figures who have the power
to move her, feed her, wash her, leave or stay
at will. And the daughter feels, with horror,
metamorphosed: *she's* such a looming figure—huge—a
                                        tower

of iron and ice—love
shrunken in her to a cube of pain
locked in her throat. O, long and long ago
she grew up and went
away and away—and now's bereft
of tears and unable
to comfort the child her mother's become.
Instead, by the bedside, briskly, nervously,
carries out doctor's orders;
                    or travelling endlessly
in the air-conditioned sameness of jet-plane efficiency,
withdraws into lonely distance
(the patient left in the best of hands).

Watering the blue ajuga in her Boston yard
she imagines her mother may, after all,
be needing her—should she have left?
Imagines her mother at six years old in the riverfield,
twelve years old in her orphan's mourning,

twenty, forty, eighty—the storied screen unfolding,
told and told—and the days untold. A life!
A life—ninetythree years unique in the aeons.
She wants to go back to Mexico, sit by her mother,
have her be strong and say, *Go, child, and I bless you.*
She did say it! But weakly; it wasn't enough; she wants
to hear it again and again.

                But she does not go back. Remembers
herself as a monstrous, tall, swift-moving nurse.
And remembers the way
she longed to leave, while she was there,
trapped in the house of strangers.
Something within her twists and turns,
she is tired and ashamed. She sobs, but her eyes
cannot make tears. She imagines herself
entering a dark cathedral to pray, and blessedly
falling asleep there, and not wakening
for a year, for seven years, for a century.

A Daughter (II)

Heading south, above
thick golden surf of cloud.
Along the western earthcurve,
eternal sunset, a gaunt red,
crouches, a wing outstretched,
immobile.
       Southward, deathward, time inside the jet
pauses. A drone of deafness—'Would you care
to purchase a cocktail?' mouthed
ritually. She clings, drink in hand,
to her isolation.

       A day later begins
the witnessing. A last week of the dying.
When she inserts
       quivering spoonfuls of violently
green or red *gelatina*
       into the poor obedient mouth,
she knows it's futile. Hour by hour
the body that bore her
shrinks and grows colder
and suffers. But days go by, and the long nights.

Each dawn the daughter, shivering,
opens the curtained door
and steps out on the balcony; and from time to time
leans there during the days. Mornings,
emphatic sunlight seizes the bougainvillea's
dry magenta blossoms. Among sharp stones, below,
of the hospital patio,
       an ugly litter of cigarette stubs
thrown down by visitors leaning, anxious or bored,
from other balconies. No one sweeps up.
Sobs shake her—no tears. She hates
the uncaring light.

Afternoons
it's better, when impetuously
the rain hurls itself earthward for an hour.
Abruptly it stops, the steep streets
are full of the voice of rivers, adobe-brown,
sky still dark for a while.

Mostly, when there's no help to be given the nurse,
no feeding, moving, changing of sheets to be done,
and vital signs have been checked once more,
she sits with her back to the light
and listens—eyes on whatever book her mind
hungrily moves in, making its way
alone, holding on—listens
to hiss of oxygen and the breathing,
still steady,
she knows will
change rhythm, change
again,
and stop.

Some force roaming the universe,
malicious and stupid, affixed, she feels,
this postscript to so vivid a life.
This tide that does not ebb, this persistence
stuck like a plane in mournful clouds,
what can it signify?
is any vision
—an entrance into a garden
of recognitions and revelations, Eden
of radiant comprehensions, taking
timeless place in the wounded head, behind
the closed, or glazed half-open, eyes?
Are words of deserved joy
singing behind the sunken lips that bent
stiffly into a formal smile when the daughter arrived again,
but now shape only *no* when pain
forces them back to speech?

There are flies in the room. The daughter
busies herself, placing wet gauze
over her mother's mouth and eyes.
                              What she wants
she knows she can't have: one minute
of communion, here in limbo.
                         All the years of it,
talk, laughter, letters. Yet something
went unsaid. And there's no place
to put whatever it was, now,
no more chance.

Even two weeks after her fall,
three weeks before she died, the garden
began to vanish. The rickety fence gave way
as it had threatened, and the children threw
broken plastic toys—vicious yellow,
unresonant red, onto the path, into the lemontree;
or trotted in through the gap, trampling small plants.
For two weeks no one watered it, except
I did, twice, but then I left. She was still conscious then
and thanked me. I begged the others to water it—
but the rains began; when I got back there were violent,
sudden, battering downpours each afternoon.
                                        Weeds flourished,
dry topsoil was washed away swiftly
into the drains. Oh, there was green, still,
but the garden was disappearing—each day
less sign of the ordered,
thought-out oasis, a squared circle her mind
constructed for rose and lily, begonia
and rosemary-for-remembrance.
Twenty years in the making—
less than a month to undo itself;
and those who had seen it grow,
living around it those decades,
did nothing to hold it. Oh, Alberto did,
one day, patch up the fence a bit,
when I told him a future tenant would value
having a garden. But no one believed
the garden-maker would live (I least of all),
so her pain if she were to see the ruin
remained abstract, an incomprehensible concept,
impelling no action. When they carried her past
                                        on a stretcher,
on her way to the *sanatorio*, failing sight
transformed itself into a mercy: certainly

32

she could have seen no more than a greenish blur.
But to me the weeds, the flowerless rosebushes, broken
stems of the canna lilies and amaryllis, all
a lusterless jungle green, presented—
even before her dying was over—
an obdurate, blind, all-seeing gaze:
I had seen it before, in the museums,
in stone masks of the gods and victims.
A gaze that admits no tenderness; if it smiles, it
only smiles with sublime bitterness—no,
not even bitter: it admits
no regret, nostalgia has no part in its cosmos,
bitterness is irrelevant.
If it holds a flower—and it does,
a delicate brilliant silky flower that blooms only
a single day—it holds it clenched
between sharp teeth.
Vines may crawl, and scorpions, over its face,
but though the centuries blunt
eyelid and flared nostril, the stone gaze
is utterly still, fixed, absolute,
smirk of denial facing eternity.
Gardens vanish. She was an alien here,
as I am. Her death
was not Mexico's business. The garden though
was a hostage. Old gods
took back their own.

Notes

PAGE
10 The West Heath is a section of Hampstead Heath, the tract of never-cultivated land that overlooks London from the north and includes the point of highest elevation in the London area.

11 'The small, dark-green volumes. / The awkward, heroic versions' refers to the English collected edition of Constance Garnett's pioneer translations.

Für Elise is a short piano piece by Beethoven.

12 'The Black Monk' is a Chekhov story often, or perhaps I should say usually, interpreted quite differently—that is, as being a sad story about illusion. I did not then, and do not now, see it that way. All the *apparent* illusion in it is in fact what is strong and positive!

13 'The betrothed girl' is the heroine of the story variously translated as 'The Betrothed,' 'A Marriageable Girl,' 'The Bride,' etc.

14 'tender, delightful, ironic'—from Gorki's reminiscences of Chekov. However, just about everyone who ever described Chekhov mentioned his smile in very similar terms.

34

CONTINUUM

i

Milk to be boiled
egg to be poached
pot to be scoured.

Bandage to bind
firm around old bones
cracked in a fall:

White hair to be brushed
cold feet to be warmed
gnarled toenails to cut.

When there is work to be done
moonwavering images
of sentiment and desire
ride away into the forest

and sexual songs
shake their preened wings
and fly off, casting
a few loose feathers

scarlet and purple

soon invisible.

ii

Over the mountains
lean the clouds
as if their shadows were mirrors.

37

Lay down poison
in the track of the ants
who devour the roses.

When there is work to do
one laughs at oneself,
the intense life of the heart
stops talking.

How frail, how small,
the body that bore me.
She too
is laughing:

'Skin and bones' she says.
'The bandage is like
a knight's armour,' she says.
'What dragons
are to be vanquished?'

She grew old.
She made ready to die.
She gave counsel to women and men, to young girls and
                                        young boys.
She remembered her griefs.
She remembered her happinesses.
She watered the garden.
She accused herself.
She forgave herself.
She learned new fragments of wisdom.
She forgot old fragments of wisdom.
She abandoned certain angers.
She gave away gold and precious stones.
She counted-over her handkerchiefs of fine lawn.
She continued to laugh on some days, to cry on others,
                    unfolding the design of her identity.
She practiced the songs she knew, her voice
                              gone out of tune
                    but the breathing-pattern perfected.
She told her sons and daughters she was ready.
She maintained her readiness.
She grew very old.
She watched the generations increase.
She watched the passing of seasons and years.
She did not die.

She did not die but lies half-speechless, incontinent,
                    aching in body, wandering in mind
                    in a hospital room.
A plastic tube, taped to her nose,
        disappears into one nostril.
Plastic tubes are attached to veins in her arms.
Her urine runs through a tube into a bottle under the bed.
On her back and ankles are black sores.

The black sores are parts of her that have died.
The beat of her heart is steady.
She is not whole.

She made ready to die, she prayed, she made her peace,
    she read daily from the lectionary.
She tended the green garden she had made,
    she fought off the destroying ants,
    she watered the plants daily
    and took note of their blossoming.
She gave sustenance to the needy.
She prepared her life for the hour of death.
But the hour has passed and she has not died.

O Lord of mysteries, how beautiful is sudden death
    when the spirit vanishes
    boldly and without casting
    a single shadowy feather of hesitation
    onto the felled body.

O Lord of mysteries, how baffling, how clueless
    is laggard death, disregarding
    all that is set before it
        in the dignity of welcome—
    laggard death, that steals
        insignificant patches of flesh—
    laggard death, that shuffles
    past the open gate,
    past the open hand,
    past the open,
            ancient,
            courteously waiting life.

Mother, when I open a book of yours
your study notes fall out into my lap.
'Apse, semicircular or polygonal recess
arched over domed roof,' says one. I remember
your ceiling, cracked by earthquake,
and left that way. Not that you chose to leave it;
nevertheless, 'There's nothing less real
than the present,' you underlined.

My throat clenches when I weep and
can't make tears,
the way my feet clenched when I ran
unsuspecting into icy ocean
for 'General swim,' visiting Nik at summercamp.
What hurts is not your absence only,
dull, unresonant, final,
it's the intimate knowledge of your aspirations,
the scholar in you, the artist reaching
out and out.
                        To strangers your unremitting
struggle to learn appears
a triumph—to me, poignant. I know
how baffled you felt.
I know only I
knew how lonely you were.
The small orphan,
skinny, proud, reserved, observant,
irreverent still in the woman of ninety,
but humble.

"To force conscience," you marked in Panofsky,
"is worse,' says Castellio, 'than cruelly
to kill a man. For to deny one's convictions
destroys the soul."
                        And Bruno's lines,

41

"The age
Which I have lived, live, and shall live,
Sets me atremble, shakes, and braces me."

Five months before you died you recalled
counting-rhymes, dance-games for me;
gaily, under the moon, you sang and mimed,

>   My shoes are very *dirty*,
>   My shoes are very *thin*,
>   I haven't got a *pocket*
>   To put a penny in.

>   *A soul-cake, a soul-cake,*
>   *Please, good missis, a soul-cake* . . .

But by then for two years
you had hardly been able to hear me,
could barely see to read.
>   We spoke together
>   less and less.

There's too much grief. Mother,
what shall I do with it?
Salt grinding and grinding from the magic box.

Ah, grief, I should not treat you
like a homeless dog
who comes to the back door
for a crust, for a meatless bone.
I should trust you.

I should coax you
into the house and give you
your own corner,
a worn mat to lie on,
your own water dish.

You think I don't know you've been living
under my porch.
You long for your real place to be readied
before winter comes. You need
your name,
your collar and tag. You need
the right to warn off intruders,
to consider
my house your own
and me your person
and yourself
my own dog.

Iron scallops border the path, barely
above the earth; a purplish starling lustre.

Earth a different dark, scumbled, bare
between clumps of wintered-over stems.

Slowly, from French windows opened
to first, mild, pale, after-winter morning,

we inch forward, looking: pausing, examining
each plant. It's boring. The dry stalks
are tall as I, up to her thigh. But then—
'Ah! Look! A snowdrop!' she cries,
satisfied, and I see

thin sharp green darning-needles
stitch through the sticky gleam of dirt,

belled with white!
                    'And another!
And here, look, and here.'
                              A white carillon.
Then she stoops to show me precise
bright green check-marks

vivid on inner petals,
each outer petal
filing down to a point.

                    And more:
'Crocuses—yes, here they are . . .'

and these point upward, closed
tight as eyelids waiting a surprise,

44

egg-yoke gold or mauve;
and she brings my gaze

to filigree veins of violet
traced upon white, that make

the mauve seem. This is the earliest
spring of my life. Last year

I was a baby, and what I saw then
is forgotten. Now I'm a child. Now I'm not bored

at moving step by step,
slow, down the path. Each pause

brings us to bells or flames.

Emblem (I)

Dreaming, I rush
thrust from the cave of the winds,
into the midst of a wood of tasks.
The boughs part, I sweep
poems and people with me a little way;
dry twigs, small patches of earth
are cleared and covered.
Then I find myself
out over open heath, a sigh that holds
a single note, heading
far and far to the horizon's bent firtree.

Emblem (II)

A silver quivering cocoon that shakes
from within, trying to break.
                          What psyche
is wrestling with its shroud?
Blunt diamonds
scrape at its casing,
urging it out.
But there is too much grief. The world
is made of days, and is itself
a shrouded day.
It stifles. It's our world, and we
its dreams, its creased
compacted wings.

Kindness

'Was it eyes of friendship the dog had?'
Robert Duncan, 1964, writing about
a poem, 'As It Happens.'

Eyes of kindness that the dog had,
the 3-legged beggar dog,
were not eyes of friendship—no:
in its hunger, dog
gave over to the stricken
heart of a watcher—not a giver—
(bereaved, an alien
for a time among the living)
agony. Shared it. As that watcher
would share a used-up bone, a crust.
In a fog of dust and grief
in the sun
the dog's hurt life
was itself
a kindness. Timidly
the beast took
the afterthought of bread.
The traveller took
in exchange
its gift
for a while, and
wept in it, enabled.

What a flimsy shred of the world
I hold by its tenuous, filmy edge!
All my multitudes,
the tribes of my years passing
    into murmurous caverns,
the grassblades, flinty paths,
words, baled reams of inscribed paper, cities,
cities recurring composite
in dream,
        skin, breath, lashes, hair,
closeups, perspectives—a hive of knowledge
no bigger than a bead of sweat.

Fish are uttering silence in the ocean's holes—
and all about me,
unconceived,
the foundries, steelmill flames aloft flaring, clangor,
the vast routine of power,
what it is to be threadbare,
breathe asbestos,
daily for fifty years to tread
certain adamantine steps,
            kill, to have killed.

Unknown lurchings into calculus, landing
the plane I fly in. And each other dreamer
clutching (wideawake) a different frayed
scrap of fabric!
        Are there gods whose pleasure
is to make rag rugs, deftly
braiding? Quilts for eternity? Needled blood
from Chthonian fingers speckling
the ritual patterns?

Scornful Reprieve

Curtly the sky
plucks
at knots of cloud;
from the unfurled bundles
out roll pellets
of leaden rain,
singly, savagely,
dropping, to pock
the pale
        dust of the earth.
Something cannot believe
a gift has been given.
Shall grass indeed
grow here?

Alongside

Catbird cadenzas from the bushes
issue like edicts. See him! Fearless,
intent upon invention, slate blue
among the dewy leaves, his puffed throat
pumping. Alongside
the human day, his day,
fully engaged.
        Miaow!
A bright glance registers
old Two-legs passing by. Not his concern,
pah! A billion leaves
demand utterance, he has the whole
hillside to sing, the veil of vapor.
Azaleas must be phrased! And dandelions—
a golden pizzicato!
Soon enough
it will be noon, and hot, and silent.

49

A brown oakleaf, left over from last year,
turns into a bird and flies off singing.

That should encourage you!   I know it—
but I'm not an oakleaf.

I'm not singing.

I'm not watching the brown wings
cleave the air.

The cold half-moon
sits obstinate in this warm, middle-of-the-day,
middle of the month.

I'm looking sullenly back at it,
human, thrown
back on my own resources.

Some trick of light

in the reflection of sunny kitchen against
a dark wall in back of the yard

makes this morning's daffodils
that shout for joy, thronging their stone vase,
leaning outward in a ring,
golden, hilarious, ready for anything,
for spring—

makes them into a cluster
of yellow chrysanthemums,
no less beautiful,
                    but very still,
facing November,
facing frost.

Through the high leafy branches
rush of wind-flood.   Gleam
of the wind's teeth
at dead of night, *calavera.*
Dark of the moon.
Under the smiling skin
bloodstream furtively
slower.   The wind sweeping aside
the weir of leaves. Meshing
of counterrhythms. So,
is this how time
takes one? Bricks returned to clay
in Nineveh? Sheba's gazebo
silted over, under
the desert tides?

The Long Way Round

for Alice Walker and Carolyn Taylor

i

'The solution,' they said to my friend,
'lies in eventual total'—they said (or 'final'?),
'assimilation. Miscegeny. No more trouble—'
            Disappear, they said.

I in America,
            white, an
                        indistinguishable mixture
of Kelt and Semite, grown under glass
in a British greenhouse, a happy
old-fashioned artist, sassy and free,

had to lean in yearning towards
the far-away daughters and sons of
Vietnamese struggle
before I could learn,
            begin to learn,
by Imagination's slow ferment,
what it is to awaken
each day Black in White America,
each day struggling
            to affirm
a who-I-am my white skin never
has to pay heed to.
            Who I am
slowly, slowly
            took lessons
from distant Asia; and only then
from near-as-my-hand persons, Black sisters.

ii

Pushing open my mind's
door on its grating hinges
to let in the smell of
pain, of destroyed
flesh, to know
                for one instant's agony,
                insisted on for the sake of knowing
                anything, anything at all
                in truth,
that that flesh belonged
to one's own most dear,
child, or lover, or mother—

pushing open my door I began
to know who I was and
who I was not.
And slowly—for though
it's in a flash we
know we know,
yet before that flash there's a long
slow, dull, movement of fire
along the well-hidden
line of the fuse—

I came to know,
                in the alembic
of grief and will and love,
just barely to know, by knowing
it never
        ever
                would be what I could
know in the flesh,

what it must be to wake each day
to the sense of one's own beautiful
human skin, hair, eyes, one's

54

whole warm sleep-caressed body
as something that others
hated,
       hunted,
              haunted by its otherness,
something they wanted to see disappear.

iii

Swimming, we are, all of us, swimming
in the rectangular indoor claustrophobic pool
—echoing, sharply smelling of chlorine,
stinging our eyes—
that is
our life,

              where,
         scared and put off our stroke
         but righting ourselves with a gasp
                   sometimes we touch
an Other,
              another
breathing and gasping body,
'yellow,' but not yellow at all,
'black,' but most often
brown; shaped like ourselves, bodies we could
embrace in relief, finding
ourselves not alone in the water.

              And someone,
                   some fool of a coach,
strutting the pool's edge, wading
the shallow end, waves his arms at us,
shouting,
         'If you're White
         you have
         the right of way!'

                        While we
swim for dear life, all of us—'not,'
as it has been said, '*not* waving,
but drowning.'

On the 32nd Anniversary
of the Bombing of Hiroshima and Nagasaki

A new bomb, big one, drops
a long way beyond the fence of our minds'
property. And they tell us, *"With this
the war is over.'*
              We are twenty years old, thereabouts—
now stale uniforms
can fall off our backs, replaced
by silk of youth! Relief,
not awe, gasps from our
mouths and widens
ignorant eyes. We've been used
to the daily recitation of death's
multiplication tables: we don't notice
the quantum leap: eighty-seven thousand
killed outright by a single bomb,
fifty-one thousand missing or injured.
We were nurses, refugees, sailors, soldiers,
familiar with many guises of death: war had ended our
                            childhood.
We knew about craters, torpedoes, gas ovens.
This we ignored.
The rumor was distant traffic. Louder
were our heartbeats,
                summer was springtime:
'The war is over!'

And on the third day no-one
rose from the dead at Hiroshima,
and at Nagasaki
the exploit was repeated, as if
to insist we take notice:
seventy-three thousand
killed by one bomb,
seventy-four thousand injured or missing.

57

Familiar simple-arithmetic of
mortal flesh did not serve,
                              yet I cannot remember,
and Sid, Ruth, Betty, Matthew, Virginia
cannot remember August sixth or
August ninth, nineteen-
forty-five. *The war was over* was all we knew
and a vague wonder, *what next? What will ordinary
life be like, now ordinary life as we know it
is gone?*

But the shadow,
the human shadowgraph sinking itself
indelibly upon stone at Hiroshima
as a man, woman or child was consumed
in unearthly fire—
                     that shadow
already had been for three days
imprinted upon our lives.
Three decades now we have lived
with its fingers outstretched in horror clinging
to our future, our children's future,
into history or the void.
The shadow's voice
cries out to us to cry out.
Its nails dig
                into our souls
                                to wake them:
'*Something,*' it ceaselessly
repeats, its silence
a whisper, its whisper
a shriek,
            while 'the radiant gist'
is lost, and the moral labyrinths of
humankind convulse as if made
of snakes clustered and intertwined and stirring
from long sleep—
'. . . *something can yet*

be salvaged upon the earth:
try, try to survive,
try to redeem
the human vision
from cesspits where human hands
have thrown it, as I was thrown
from life into shadow. . . .'

It was a land where the wingéd mind
could alight.
Andean silver dazzling the Southern Cross;
the long shore of gold beaten by the Pacific
into translucency, vanishing
into Antarctica—
                    yes, these:
          but not for these
our minds flew there,

but because they knew
the poor were singing there
and the homeless
were building there
and the downtrodden
were dancing.

How brief it was, that time
when Chile showed us how to rejoice!
How soon the executioners
arrived, making victims
of those who were not born to be victims.

The throats of singers
were punched into silence,
hands of builders
crushed,
dancers herded
into the pens.

               How few
all over the earth,
from pole to pole, are the lands
where our minds can perch and be glad,
clapping their wings, a phoenix flock!

From Chile now
they fly affrighted, evil smoke
rises from forest and city,
hopes are scorched.

When will the cheerful hammers sound again?
When will the wretched begin to dance again?
When will guitars again
give forth at the resurrected touch
of broken fingers
a song of revolution reborn?

Our large hands
Your small hands

Our country's power
Our powerlessness against it

Your country's poverty
The power of your convictions

Our corrupted democracy
The integrity of your revolution

Our technology and its barbarity
Your ingenuity and simple solutions

Our bombers
Your bicycles

Our unemployed veterans
Your re-educated prostitutes

Our heroin addicts rotting
Your wounded children healing

Our longing for new life
Your building of new life

Our large hands
Your small hands

Some beetle trilling
its midnight utterance.

Voice of the scarabee,
dungroller,
working survivor . . .

I recall how each year
returning from voyages, flights
over sundown snowpeaks,
cities crouched over darkening lakes,
hamlets of wood and smoke,
I find
        the same blind face upturned to the light
        and singing
        the one song,

        the same weed managing
        its brood of minute stars
        in the cracked flagstone.

PAGE
58   shadowgraph—this is factual and may be viewed at Hiroshima.

MODULATIONS FOR SOLO VOICE

These poems were written in the winter and spring of 1974–75, and might be subtitled, from the cheerful distance of 1978, *Historia de un amor*. They are intended to be read as a sequence.

There are the lover and the beloved, but these two come from different countries.
Carson McCullers
The Ballad of the Sad Café

The world is round.
Amber beads
I took from around my neck
before we lay down, before
you left to go onward and homeward,
remind me, and the saying:
'Each place on earth is
the middle of the world."

A certain blue would be
your color, no? Dark
as your irises
that ringed black tarns
I looked into,
           that looked
back at me,
gaze holding.

                 .

I could sail around the world looking
for your country
and never find it—what would it mean to me
unless you were in it,
it is you I want, to look
with love into me,
to come into me,
you who came out of the
bluest furthest distance.
Who left so soon, going
inexorably
north into snow,
           like a messenger gone into Lapland
           with runes for the watchful sages,
           with gentleness wrapped in linen to give
           their crystal princess
           under those stern auroras.

I wanted to learn you by heart.
There was only time
for the opening measures—a minor key,
major chords, arpeggios of desire that ripple
             swifter than I can hum them—
and through all
a lucid, dreaming tune
that gleaners sing
alone in the fields.

I am wayfaring
in the middle of the world,
treading water, the blue
of your absence,
cold ocean; trudging
the dusty earth-curves
to unending distance,
round and round.
Listening for that music,
singing within me
the first notes over,
as if in the middle of the
round world you could hear me?

i

Halfawake, I think
silky hair, cornsilk, his voice
of one substance with
his words, with
his warm flesh.
I put my hand out
in the dark to touch
his letter, placed
in reach for the night's
shoals of waking.
What I know of him
is a flow unbroken
from word to touch,
from body to thought's
dance or stillness.
Therefore into my palm
off the paper
rises what soothes me,
indivisible;
I can return
into the sea of sleep.

ii

Today the telephone
brought me his voice itself:
the silk of it
is darker than I remembered,
and warmer.
I took the folds of it up
to wrap myself in,
to keep off the cold of
all the snowfields between us.

Big bluejay black,
white sky in back; brittle;
twisting bare random
branches.   Morning
persists in rain, rain
that last night
dripped from the eaves
in pacing footsteps.
Awake and awake
I was ashamed:
only lonely private sorrows
took my sleep—
(*only lonely, only lonely* . . . as if a child
sat in a treehouse,
moping). Politics,
the word I use to mean
striving for justice and for
mercy, never
keeps me so long
open-eyed. The world's
crowded with crowded
prisons; if Debs
was truthful, humankind
can feel more than
I know or
for more than a moment
can sustain. What turns
the jay blue
again in gray
rainlight is not,
this morning, news
of any justice or freedom
but (o infinitesimal,
fragile, vast, only!)
the mercy of one voice

70

speaking from far away
lowpitched, loving,
one to one . . .

I am angry with X, with Y, with Z,
for not being you.
Enthusiasms jump at me,
wagging and barking. Go away.
Go home.

I am angry with my eyes for not seeing you,
they smart and ache and see the snow,
an insistent brilliance.

If I were Psyche how could I not
bring the lamp to our bedside?
I would have known in advance
all the travails my gazing
would bring, more than Psyche
ever imagined,
and even so, how could I not have raised
the amber flame to see
the human person I knew
was to be revealed.
She did not even know! She dreaded
a beast and discovered
a god. But I
know, and hunger
to witness again the form
of mortal love itself.

I am angry with everything that is filling
the space of your absence,
breathing your air.
                    Psyche,
how blessed you were
in the dark, knowing him in your flesh:
I was wrong! If I were Psyche
I would live on in darkness, and endure

72

the foolish voices, barking of aeolian dogs,
                                    the desert glitter
of days full of boring treasures,
walking on precious stones till my feet hurt,

to hold you each night and be held
close in your warmth in a pitchblack cave of a room

and not have to wait
for Mercury, dressed in the sad gray coat of a mailman
and no wings on his feet,
to bring me your words.

A Woman Pacing Her Room, Rereading a Letter, Returning Again and Again to Her Mirror

i

Poised on the edge of ugliness,

a flower whose petals
are turning brown.
          I never liked
to keep them—a word of farewell
discreetly whispered, and out they go,
the discolored water after them,
the vase to be scrubbed.
          A few flowers
dry into straw-crisp comeliness
without fetor. But
for most
        beauty is balanced upon
the poignance of brevity.

I have almost fallen already,
an ordinary flower.
But my lover talks about two years from now . . .
In two years I may be richly
gone into compost—juice and fiber
absorbed in the dark of
time past, my fever
a flame remembered,
              old candle,
              old shadow.
Or in two years I may be straw.

          Flowers of straw,
everlastings, are winter makeshifts
pleasant to see, but not to touch.
Their voice is a faint crackling under the hand.

By spring the settled
              dust is dull
                            upon brittleness,

              and someone brings in
posies of fragrance from the meadows,
violets, the forgotten, now-to-be-known-freshly
primrose;
              dew is on them,
              what could one ever
              desire but to sink with closed eyes
              into their cold, sweet, brief,
              silent music?

**ii (The Woman Has Ceased to Pace, She Sits Down on the
Edge of Her Bed, Still Holding the Letter)**

We can't save
our tears in precious vials,
or if we do, we don't know
what to do with them then,
iridescent amphorae
              coated with salt . . .
                            We can't save
ourselves, I cannot hold
my fleeting, fading, ordinary hedgerow rays
                            of sun or star homage
from falling, from leaving
              nothing but the small nub they flare from
—and that itself
swiftly or slowly must turn
from gold to mole-dark gray.

Dream: Château de Galais

In dream you ask me
to care for your child while its mother
rides in the tapestry forest.
The whole château

is thronged with fair and strange
folk, both Frantz de Galais and his friends, and
your friends, my friends, and many
personages without whom my story
would have been a blank.

I lie down beside the child
to lull her to sleep, and I lull myself
to sleep. A remote attic, daytime, a room
where perhaps the godmother sometimes
                                sits at her spinning.

And when I awake, the belovéd
rosy and longlashed daughter, fragrant
with infant sweat, is curled
confidingly into my circling protective arm,
and you have entered the room

searching for me, for now at last
we can meet alone for an hour.
Smiling, your hand on the door, eager to leave.
It is a subtle and delicate task to rise
so softly she will not wake.
Tendrils of hair, silky like yours,
cling damp to my cheek
where her head nestles.
But you want me. You take my hands,

we steal from the safe room quickly.
This was a dream
of sadness, of sleep, of a place
known to our minds, of seeking each other,
of joy.

76

Like Loving Chekhov

Loving this man who is far away
is like loving Anton Chekhov.
It is true, I do love Anton Chekhov,
I have loved him longer than I have known this man.
I love all the faces of Chekhov in my collection
of photos that show him in different years of his life,
alone, or with brothers and sisters, with actors,
with Gorki,
with Tolstoi, with his wife, with his undistinguished
endearing pet dogs; from beardless student to pince-nez'd
famous and ailing man.
I have no photo
of the man I love.

I love Chekhov for travelling alone
to the prison island without being asked.
For writing of the boiling, freezing, terrible seas
around the island and around the lives of its people
that they 'resembled the scared dreams
of a small boy who's been reading
Lost in the Ocean Wastes
before going to sleep, and whose blanket has fallen off,
so he huddles shivering
and can't wake up.'
For treasuring the ugly inkstand a penniless seamstress
gave him in thanks for his doctoring.
If there's an afterlife,
I hope to meet Anton Chekhov there.

Loving the man I love
is like that, because he is far away,
and because he is scrupulous, and because surely
nothing he says or does can bore me.
But it's different too. Chekhov had died
long before I was born. This man is alive.

He is alive and not here.
This man has shared my bed, our bodies
have warmed each other and given each other
delight, our bodies
are getting angry with us for giving them to each other
and then
allowing something they don't understand to
pry them apart,
a metallic
cruel wedge that they hear us call
necessity.
       Often it seems unreal to love
a man who is far away, or only real to the mind,
the mind teasing the body. But it's real,
he's alive, and it's not in the afterlife
I'm looking to see him,
but in this here and now, before I'm a month older,
before one more gray hair has grown on my head.
If he makes me think about Chekhov it's not because
he resembles him in the least but because the ache
of distance between me and a living man I know and
don't know
grips me with pain and fear, a pain and fear
familiar in the love of the unreachable dead.

'My delicate Ariel'—
can you imagine,
Caliban had a sister?
Not ugly, brutish, wracked with malice,
but nevertheless
earthbound half-sibling to him,
and, as you once were,
prisoned within a tree—
but that tree being
no cloven pine but the sturdy wood
her body seemed to her,
its inner rings revealing
slow growth,
its bark incised
with hearts and arrows,
all its leaves wanting to fly, and falling—
     and ever in spring again
     peering forth small as flint-sparks?

Spirit whose feet touch earth
only as spirit moves them,
imagine
     this rootbound woman,
Prospero's bastard daughter,
his untold secret, hidden from Miranda's
gentle wonder.
     Her intelligent eyes
watch you, her mind
can match your own, she loves
your grace of intellect.
But she knows
what weight of body is, knows her flesh
(her cells, her magic cell)
mutters its own dark songs.

She loves

to see you pass by,
grieves that she cannot hold you,
knows it is so and *must* be;
offers the circle of her shade,
silvery Ariel,
for your brief rest.

Modulations

'The laws of modulation are found in *The Science of Harmony*,
which treats of the formation and progression of chords.'
Simple & Complete Primer for the Pianoforte, 1885

i

Easily we are happy, I was thinking, no need
for so much grieving,
ashen mind, heart flaming, flaming
from core of stone.

Easy days, nights when our bodies
were learning each other.

ii

But that perfection, nectarine of light—
you bruised it.
Impeccably conscientious,
gave it a testing pinch,

reminding me of my status
in the country of your affections:
secondclass citizen.

Don't you know I hate to be told
what I know already?
Remember the custodian telling us,
'This chair is beautiful,
this is a beautiful table'?
What I knew I'd taken already
on terms of my own:
not as defeat but with new freedom—
            from false pride,
            from measuring my value to you
            in a jeweller's finicky scale.

(And *the heart's affections* are *holy,*
we have known that, but have loved
to hear it again for the sake of
his life who said it. And *what the Imagination seizes
as beauty must be truth—*
yet there are hierarchies within that truth.)

iii

*Nectarine of our pleasure,
enclosed in its own fragrance,
poised on its imaginary branch!*
I imagine too quickly, giving to tenuous things
hasty solidity,
to irresolute shadows
a perfect equilibrium.

For you, then,
our days and nights had not been a river
flowing at leisure between grassy banks?

You thought I would try
to force the river
out of its course?

You didn't trust me . . .

iv

Or perhaps indeed
we did after all
share our pleasure,
halving the nectarine—

but even as we drifted
downstream at ease

and golden juices
stained your mind's tongue,

Anxiety arrived from your hometown
wearing black,
waving her umbrella?

v

Since I must recover
my balance, I do. I falter
but don't fall; recalling
how every vase, cut sapphire, absolute
dark rose, is not indeed
of rarest, of most cherished
perfection unless flawed,
offcentered, pressed
with rough thumbprint, bladescratch, brown
birthmark that tells
of concealed struggle from bud to open ease
of petals, soon
to loosen, to drop and
be blown away.
                    The asymmetrical
tree of life, fractionally lopsided
at the trunk's live-center
tells where a glancing eye,
                    not a ruler,
drew, and drew strength
from its mistake.

The picture of perfection
must be revised.
Allow for our imperfections,
welcome them,
consume them into its substance.
Bring from necessity

its paradoxical virtue,
mortal life, that makes it
give off so strange a magnetic
shining, when one had thought
darkness had filled the night.

vi

These questions
that have walked beside all that I say,
waiting their turn for utterance:

> How do I free myself
> from pain self-imposed,

>> pride-pain,
>> will-pain,

>> pain of wanting
>> never to feel superfluous?

> How are you acted on
> by anxiety, by a coldness
> taught to you as a boy?

—these questions
are not mine only.
The vision

of river, of nectarine,

is not mine only.
All humankind,

women and men,

hungry,

84

hungry beyond the hunger
for food, for justice,

pick themselves up and stumble on
for this: to transcend barriers, longing

for absolution of each by each,
luxurious unlearning
of lies and fears,

for joy, that *throws down the reins*
on the neck of
             the divine animal
who carries us through the world.

High on vitamins, I demonstrate to my friends
the *lezginka, mazurka, gavotte.* With a
one two three, hop, one two three, hop, teach
someone the polka.
                            Laughter's a joy
even next day at breakfast.
Do I really suffer
that his letters arrive so seldom—
unwritten or unmailed?
Is it love or pride that hurts?
Am I maybe
fully as jocund as I seem?

(Only twice I've cried
in weeks now—once
writing of my mother's
extreme old age, the slow
race between heart and sight;
once when I read about Li-li's
lost first love, when her parents
pulled her away to Taiwan,
away from her comrades.
Did they die in the struggle against Chiang Kai-shek?)

Is 'the fine art of unhappiness' truly
losing its allure?

*The first poem
becomes the last.*

The world
is round.
I am wayfaring.

I learned
the tense and slender
warmth of your body
almost by heart.

The bluest, furthest distance
is what you carry
within you—
the cold of it
inexorable.

I know
you can't hear me.

I'm gleaning
alone in a field
in the middle of the world,

you're listening
for a song that
I don't know,

that no one
yet has sung.

*This is not
farewell.
I have*

your word for it,
inviolate.
The last poem

enclosed in the lucid
amber of the world

becomes the first.

I thought I had found a swan
but it was a migrating snow-goose.

I thought I was linked invisibly to another's life
but I found myself more alone with him than without him.

I thought I had found a fire
but it was the play of light on bright stones.

I thought I was wounded to the core
but I was only bruised.

PAGE
70 Debs—Eugene V. Debs, who declared in a speech in court on September 11, 1918: '. . . while there is a lower class, I am in it; while there is a criminal element, I am of it; while there is a soul in prison, I am not free.'

76 'Dream: Château de Galais'—refers to Alain-Fournier's *Le Grand Meaulnes (The Wanderer)*.

85 *'the divine animal/who carries us through the world.'* Ralph Waldo Emerson, *The Poet:* '. . . beyond the energy of [the] possessed and conscious intellect [one] is capable of a new energy (as of an intellect doubled on itself,) by abandonment to the nature of things. . . . As a traveller who has lost his way throws his reins on his horse's neck and trusts to the instinct of the animal to find his road, so must we do with the divine animal who carries us through this world.'

ADMIRING A WATERFALL

The way sorrow enters the bone
is with stabs and hoverings.
From a torn page
a cabriolet
approaches over the crest of a hill,
first the nodding, straining head of the horse
then the blind lamps, peering;

the ladies within the insect eagerly
look from side to side awaiting the vista—
and quick as a knife
are vanished. Who were they? Where is the hill?

Or from stoked fires of nevermore
a warmth constant as breathing hovers out
to surround you, a cloud of mist
becomes rain, becomes cloak, then skin.

The way sorrow enters the bone
is the way fish sink through dense lakes
raising smoke from the depth
and flashing sideways in bevelled
syncopations.
It's the way the snow
drains the light from day but then,
covering boundaries of road and sidewalk,
widens wondering streets
and stains the sky yellow
to glow at midnight.

Listen: the wind in new leaves
whispers, smoother than fingertips,
than floss silk smoothing through fingertips . . .

When the sighted
talk about *white* they may mean
silence of sullen cold, that winter—
no matter how warm your rooms
—waits with at the door.
(Though there's another whiteness,
more like the weightlessness of a flake of snow,
of a petal, a pine-needle . . .)

When they say *black* they may mean the persistence
of cold wind hopelessly, angrily,
tearing and tearing through leafless boughs.
(Though there's another blackness,
round and full as the notes of cello and drum . . .)

But this:
this lively, delicate shiver
that whispers itself caressingly
over our flesh
when leaves are moist and small
and winds are gentle,
is green. Light green. Not weightless,
light.

Twice now this woman for whom my unreasonable dislike
has slowly turned to loathing
has come up to me and said, 'Ah, yes,
we shall have plenty of time soon to talk.'

Twice she has laid her cold hand heavily
on mine,
and thrust her pallid face, her puffy cheeks,
close to mine.
I went to wash in the hottest water, to oil myself
in fragrant oils.

I know who she is in the world; others know her;
many seem not to notice she brings
a chill into rooms.
She is who she is,
ordinary, venal, perhaps sad.
Perhaps she is not aware of her own task:
but death sends her about the world.

I have always been afraid of pain
but not of death.
I am not afraid of death, but I don't want
to have time
to sit and talk with this woman.

I have watched her condescend
to those who don't know her name,
and smirk at the ones who do.
I have seen her signature
hiding under pebbles,
scratched into chips of ice.

She can have nothing to tell me
I could be glad to hear.

Twice she has looked at me
with eyes that gleam dull, a pewter gray.
Twice she has looked at me with a look
that gives me nothing I shall ever want.

Death is for everyone. I shall never willingly
give her the right to bring me my share.
I shall refuse to take what is mine
from her gray hands.

A Look at the Night (Temple, Early '60's)

The plough
the only constellation we are
sure of

turning
the sky's earth, faithful
among its furrows of wind—

And the fierce moon
a barn-owl, over
boughs and
bright clouds—

No one

       will speak for us
       no one
       but ourselves knows
       what our lives
       are.
       We step outdoors at
       2 a.m., our minds
       dilated by deep
       early sleep,
to the quick of
             brilliant night
alone:
such words as
carry our testimony
          singular,
          incontrovertible,
          breath and tongue awaiting
          patent,
or do without.

We sing
in mutterings
to speak for ourselves.
        The turned field
black above us,
            the moon
high in her dominion.

My wedding-ring lies in a basket
as if at the bottom of a well.
Nothing will come to fish it back up
and onto my finger again.
                          It lies
among keys to abandoned houses,
nails waiting to be needed and hammered
into some wall,
telephone numbers with no names attached,
idle paperclips.
                 It can't be given away
for fear of bringing ill-luck.
              It can't be sold
for the marriage was good in its own
time, though that time is gone.
              Could some artificer
beat into it bright stones, transform it
into a dazzling circlet no one could take
for solemn betrothal or to make promises
living will not let them keep? Change it
into a simple gift I could give in friendship?

A flamey monster—plumage and blossoms
    fountaining forth
           from her round head,
    her feet
       squeezing mud between their toes,
    a tail of sorts
        wagging hopefully
    and a heart of cinders and dreamstuff,
        flecked with forever molten gold,
    drumrolling in her breast—
bore a son.

        His father? A man
not at ease with himself,
half-monster too,
half earnest earth,
        fearful of monsterhood;
        kindly, perplexed, a fire
        smouldering.

The son
    took, from both monsters, feathers
    of pure flame,

    and from his mother,
           alchemical gold,
    and from his father,
           the salt of earth:

    a triple goodness.

If to be artist
is to be monster,
he too was monster. But from his self
uprose a new fountain,

of wisdom, of in-seeing, of wingéd justice
flying unswerving
into the heart.

        He and compassion
were not master and servant,
     servant and master,
but comrades in pilgrimage.

This person would be an animal.
This animal would be large, at least as large
as a workhorse. It would chew cud, like cows,
having several stomachs.
No one could follow it
into the dense brush to witness
its mating habits. Hidden by fur,
its sex would be hard to determine.
Definitely it would discourage
investigation. But it would be, if not teased,
a kind, amiable animal,
confiding as a chickadee. Its intelligence
would be of a high order,
neither human nor animal, elvish.
And it would purr, though of course,
it being a house, you would sit in *its* lap,
not it in yours.

Artist to Intellectual (Poet to Explainer)

i

'The lovely *obvious!* The feet
supporting the body's tree and its crown
of leafy flames, of fiery
knowledge roaming
into the eyes,
that are lakes, wells, open
skies! The lovely
evident, revealing
everything, more mysterious
than any
clueless inscription scraped in stone.
The ever-present, constantly vanishing,
carnal enigma!'

ii

'Do I prophesy? It is
for now, for no future.
Do I envision? I envision
what every seed
knows, what shadow
speaks unheard
and will not repeat.
My energy
has not direction,
tames no chaos,
creates, consumes, creates
unceasing its own
wildfires that none
shall measure.'

'Don't want to measure, want to be
the worm slithering wholebodied
over the mud and grit of what
may be a mile,
may be forever—pausing
under the weeds to taste
eternity, burrowing
down not along,
rolling myself
up at a touch, outstretching
to undulate in abandon to exquisite rain,
returning, if so I desire, without
reaching that goal the measurers
think we must head for. Where is
my head? Am I not
worm all over? My own
orient!'

The Poet Li Po Admiring a Waterfall

*Improvisation on a Xmas card for the
composer David del Tredici, at Yaddo,
Xmas, 1975*

And listening to its
Japanese blues, the bass
of its steady plunging
tones of dark,
and within their roaring:
strands of thin
foamwhite, airbright
light inwoven!—all
falling
so far
so deep,
his two
acorn-hatted infant
acolytes fear
he will long to
fly like spray
and fall too, off
the sloping, pale
edge of the world,
entranced!

The sunshine is wild here!
It laps our feet!
Wavelets of sunshine!
Spiky wavelets!
The sunshine snaps at our toes!
Thick handfuls of sunshine freeze
our fingers like ice,
like burning ice cream!
Farewell!
The towers of the city across
the gulf of sunshine are wavering!

Hidden Monsters at the Mount Auburn Cemetery.
A Found Poem.

I looked after the carving while it was executing at
                                                    the prison,
and found it necessary to make only one slight deviation
                                                    from the model.
You may recollect that in most of the Egyptian cornices
there is on each side of the globe, a fabulous sort
                                                    of animal,
with an inflated body, and a head like a serpent or
                                                    crocodile . . .
As it was suggested that an uncouth Egyptian idol
might give offense to some persons,
I sought for some way of modifying it,
which might cover this difficulty
without departing from the main design.
I accordingly instructed the workmen to introduce
an Egyptian Lotus on each side,
the flower of which falls so as to conceal
the head of the monster,

leaving the spectator to imagine what he pleases behind it.

Dr. Jacob Bigelow to H.A.S. Dearborn,
Boston, January 13th, 1833

Behind the Tree the hands
of Eve and Adam almost
                        meet.
Only a single thick
rope of serpent
divides them.

Adam holds
his other hand on his heart
                        in fear
as Eve stretches out *her* other hand
across the front of the Tree
        to offer him knowledge.
The apple the serpent holds in its mouth
and the twin apples of her breasts are all
exact replicas of the apple she holds.

Four prehensile, elegant, practical feet
stand among roots.
Above the heads
                of man and woman and serpent,
dense leaves and a crown of apples hide
the font and its bas-relief stories—
        the sky's dome
upturned, an unknown cosmos.

For X . . .

I've never written poems for you, have I.
You rarely read poems,
your mind thrives
on other fruits and grains:

but just this once
a poem; to say:

As unthought gestures, turns of
common phrase, reveal
the living of life—
pathos, courage, comedy;

as in your work you witness
and show others
people's ordinary and always strange
histories;

so you give me from myself
an open secret,

a language other than my language, poetry,
in which to rest myself with you,

in which to laugh with you;

a cheerful privacy
like talking Flemish on a bus in Devon.

Love Poem

What you give me is

the extraordinary sun
splashing its light
                        into astonished trees.

A branch
of berries, swaying

under the feet of a bird.

I know
other joys—they taste
bitter, distilled as they are
from roots, yet I thirst for them.

But you—
you give me

the flash of golden daylight
in the body's
midnight,
warmth of the fall noonday
between the sheets in the dark.

Cloudy luminous rose-mallow sundown,
                              suffusing the whole
roof-and-branch-interrupted lofty
air, blue fishscale slates,
wires, poles, trolleycars, flash
of window,
rectangular Catholic tall campanile abstracted
above North Cambridge, people heads down
leaving the store with groceries, bathed—
all!—utterly
              in this deepening, poised,
              fading-to-ivory oxbowed river of
light,
one drop
of crimson lake to a brimming
floodwater chalice
and we at the lees of it—ah,
no need to float, to long
to float upward, into it, sky itself
is floating us into the dusk, we are motes
of gold brushed from the fur
of mothwings, night is
breathing
close to us,
dark, soft.

108 'Blake's Baptismal Font'—the font, in St. James's, Piccadilly, is one of Grinling Gibbons's few works in marble.

For Jon:
•
Brother in dream
•
Sometime lover
•
Friend
•
Imaginer
•

Towards not being
anyone else's center
of gravity.
            A wanting
to love: not
to lean over towards
an other, and fall,
but feel within one
a flexible steel
upright, parallel
to the spine but
longer, from which to stretch;
one's own
grave springboard; the outflying spirit's
vertical trampoline.

Spirit has been alone
of late. Built a house
of fallen leaves
among exposed tree-roots.
Plans dreamily
to fetch water

from a stone well.
Sleeps
hungrily.
        Waking,
is mute,
listening. Spirit
doesn't know
what the sound will be,
song or cry.
Perhaps

one word. Holds
at heart a
red thread, winding

back to the world,

to one who holds
the far end,
far off.
        Spirit
throws off the quilts
when darkness
is very heavy,

shuffles among
the leaves
upstairs and down

waiting
       Wants
the thread to vibrate

again. Again! Crimson!

Meanwhile refuses
visitors, asks
those who come
no questions,
answers none. Digs in
for winter,
        slowly.

The woman whose hut was mumbled by termites
—it would have to go,
  be gone,
  not soon, but some day:
  she knew it and shrugged—
had friends among the feathers,
quick hearts.

And among crickets too,
brown and faithful,
creviced at hearthside winters.

But her desire
fixed on a chrysalis.

                    How Eternity's
silver blade filed itself fine
on the whetstone of her life!
                    How the deep velours
of the wings, the mystery of the feelers,
                    drew amazed cries from her
when the butterfly came forth
and looked at her, looked at her, brilliantly gazing.
                    It was a man, her own size,
and touched her everywhere.

And how, when Time, later,
once the Eternal had left to go wandering,
knocked and knocked on her door, she smiled,
                    and would not open!

The trees
began to come in of themselves, evenings.
The termites labored.
The hut's green moss of shadows

118

gave harbor
to those who sheltered her.

She was marked
by the smile within her. Its teeth
bit and bit at her sense of loss.

You in your house among your roommate's plants
that seem at times, you tell me, an overgrown thicket
                                    of assertive leaves,
obtrusive—

are lonely. Deeply,
with a plumb-line
stillness.
            I feel it,
two miles away.

You work, your typewriter clatters cheerfully,
scenes evolve; while Dylan sings on,
                            and the record-changer
proceeds with its duties.
But underneath all is that stillness.
You hear your own heartbeats.

                            And I in my house
of smaller plants, many books, colored rugs,
my typewriter silent,
                    have been searching out for you,
though I forget how we came to speak of it, the name
of the three beings who shared
just the one fateful eye between them,
spitefully taking turns. I found them:
they were the Graiae, the Grey ones, who guarded
their sisters the Gorgons. Perseus outwitted them,
the hero who rescued Andromeda; he stole
that sinister vigilant marble, using the craftiness
that is given to heroes in time of need.

Also I found (looking for something else)
in the long, grown-up, valedictory poem
close to the end of *A Child's Garden of Verses*—

120

yes, in that elegy,
not in the black shadows of a drawing memory collaged
from the illustrations to earlier pages—
                              I found
Babylon, and candles,
                    and the long night.

I too today,
the wind and the rain transforming
my house to an island, a bare rock in the sea,
am alone
and know I'm alone,
                    silent within the gusting weather.
The plumb-line
doesn't swing, it
comes to rest

a cold small weight
hung from its faithful cord
level with heart's core.

i

The iris hazel, pupils
large in their round blackness,
his eyes
do see me,
he hugs me
tightly, but

he turns away,
he takes his grief
home with him,
my half of it
hides behind me as I
wave, he waves,
and it and I
close my door for the night.

ii

He has taken his sorrow
away to strangers.
They form a circle around it,
listening, touching,
drawing it forth.

It weeps among them,
begins to shed
cloaks and shawls, its old
gray and threadbare twisted bandages,
and show
pale skin, dark wounds.

My arms are empty,
my warm bed's empty,
I say no
to the lovers who want to warm themselves
in me.
    I want

to lie alone, dreaming awhile
about that ring dance,
that round
I don't know how to sing,
that language
strangers talk to him in,
speaking runes to his sorrow.

By the fire light
of Imagination, brand
held high in the pilgrim's
upraised hand, he sees,
not knowing what boundaries it may have,

a well, a pool or river—
water's darkly shining
mirror, offering
his sought-for Self.

O, he silently
cries out, reaching gladly.
But *O,* again: he sees
dimly, beside the knowledge
he has sought, another:

now he hesitates—
she whose face attentively
looks from the water up to him,
tutelary spirit of this place,
of the water-mirror,

who is she. It is
not a question.
It is a question
and troubles him. The flames

flutter and fail, Imagination
falters. His image
vanishes, he is left
in a vague darkness.

Then it is
he fears the glimmering presence,

her image
vanished like his own,
yet not utterly. Only

when with his breath
he reawakens fire, the light
of vision, will he once more

know the steady look, the face
of his own life. Only in presence
of his Self
can he look gladly
at that other face,

the mirror's gazing spirit,
mute, eloquent, weak, a power,
powerless,
yet giving
what he desires, if he gives light.

Part I—December

A child, no-one to stare, I'd run full tilt to a tree,
hug it, hold fast, loving the stolid way it
stood there, girth
arms couldn't round,
                         the way
only the wind made it speak, gave it
an autumn ocean of thoughts
creaking on big wings into the clouds, or rolling
in steady uncountable sevens in
to the wild cliffs when I shut my eyes.

. . . .

If I came to a brook, off came my shoes,
looking could not be enough—
or my hands at least must be boats or fish for a minute,
to know the purling water at palm and wrist.
My mind would sink like a stone
and shine underwater,
dry dull brown
                         turned to an amber glow.

. . . .

My friend . . . My friend, I would like
to talk to myself about you: beginning
with your bright, hazel, attentive eyes,
the curving lines of your mouth.
I would like to ponder the way
I have grown so slowly aware those lines
are beautiful, generous. Energy lights your
whole face, matching
the way you walk. A gradual seeing,
not in a phantom flash of storm . . .

But I'm not ready
to speak about you,
Not yet.
Perhaps I will never be ready,
nor you to be spoken of.

. . . .

Whether or not I find
words for you, to tell myself who you are,

I shan't mistake you
for a tree to cling to. Let me speak of you
as of a river:
quick-gleaming, conjuring
little pyramids of light that pass
in laughter from braided ripple to ripple;
but pausing, dark
in pools where boughs
lean over;
but never
at a standstill—

. . . .

       I don't know how deep,
how cold. I want
to touch it, drink of it, open mouth
bent to it.

Sometimes as a child
I'd slip on the rocks and fall in.
Never mind.
I wanted to know
the river's riveriness with my self,

be stone or leaf, sink or be
swept downstream

to spin and vanish, spin
and hover, spin
and sweep on beyond sight.

Part II—February

'And what if the stream
is shallow?'

Then I will wade in it.

'—the current only a ripple
that will not bear you?'

I'll make my way,
not leaf nor stone, a human,
step by step, walking,
slipping, scrambling,
seeking the depth

where the waters will summon themselves
to lift me
off my feet.

I am looking always
for the sea.

. . . .

Let me say
it is I who am a river.
Someone
is walking along
the shore of me.

He is looking

sometimes at my surface,
the lights and the passing
wingshadows,

sometimes
through me, and down
towards rocks and sand,

sometimes across me
into another country.

Does he see me?

. . . .

I met a friend
as I walked by the river that runs
through my mind.

Or he himself
was the river,

for this river
rises in metamorphosis
when some confluence
of wills occurs far-off,
            where the gods are,

and could appear
as a man,
as my friend—

who would be unaware
then, of his river-nature,

his own eyes (not
hazel, as I thought,
but topaz, are they?)
fixed rather upon flames,

for it may be
fire, not a river flowing,
flickers and glows in his mind,

while to me, drawn
to water by the pull
of searching roots,

he would seem
a river, or a man
gazing searchingly
into the river,
a fellow-wanderer . . .

Part III—April

But what are
        the trees to which—
        (to whom, were they not beings,
        impassive but sentient? 'Dreamy, gloomy,
        friendly . . .')
                —I ran long ago, and still
when I'm alone, embrace sometimes, shyly,
not impulsively: pensively;
    what within me or in those I love, or who draw me
towards themselves (as water
is pulled by roots out of the soil, to rise up
up, and up
        into the tower of the tree)
—what is the counterpart, then,
in these or myself,
to imagined, retrieved, pines and oaks of the past
uttering ocean on inland gusts of autumnal wind?
(Eyes closed, eyes closed,
            swaying as they swayed,
        listening with the heart to envisioned breakers,
the senses confounded, my breathing

130

breathing with boughs' tossing
until delight
broke in me into a dance,
unwitnessed, secret, whirling,
as if I became
a heap of firstfallen leaves
                    to eddy and fly
joyfully over the field
and scatter—)
What within us is tree?
                    What
cannot be budged, the stock
'not moved' that stands and yet
draws us
          into ourselves, centers us,
          never rebuffs us, utters
our wildest dreams for us, dreams
of oceanic blessing,
our hymns of pure being?

. . . .

Neither mighty tree,
                    sounding
                              of ocean
nor river flooding toward
                    sea-depths;

my self is a grey-barked sapling
of a race that needs
                    a hundred years' growth
close to water.
              Its dryad soul
dreams of plunging, of
swallow-diving off the pliant
twigs of its crown
into fathomless caverns, sliding
through yielding glass.

131

Its roots
        inch their toes
toward hidden streamlets
planning to pull them
                drop by drop
up through clay, gravel, thick
topsoil, to slake
                sip by sip
tree-thirst, flesh of wood that harbors
that dreamer.

. . . .

Are you flame among the branches,
unaware? You move flickering, swift, restless
in your own life,
but I see no path behind you
of blackened leaves.
                Yourself, is it,
you burn?

. . . .

Friend,
        more than friend,
                less than friend,
in dream I came to the home of your family
to deliver a message.
Messenger of the gods, I knew
nothing of what I was to tell. Only those
who received it would comprehend
what it was.
                You had a sister,
who resembled you—
                tall, curly-haired, with an aquiline, questing nose,
a sharp-edged presence, restless, charged
with some half-concealed wistful desire—
but resembled me too,

132

as if she and I were sisters: I knew this
though I know little of my own
presence, what it is.
                              She was kind to me,
welcomed me warmly into the house
which was stirring with eager people, cousins,
                                        grandparents,
aunts and uncles, all talking quickly,
                              moving through the rooms.
Everywhere green plants hung from baskets,
swaying in fish-swift ripples of light
as the family passed to and fro
smiling, vehement, pursuing
shining ribbons of concept that crisscrossed in mid-air
like strong fibers of gossamer.
I could not see you
though you were surely there
somewhere in that place where it was clear you belonged;
but your sister drew me kindly into the midst
and brought me the cup that is brought
to messengers from distant places, before they must
                                        speak.

. . . .

I see for sure now
        beginning to speak of you, ready,
        for a moment's grace, to speak at last
        of what I don't know but see in the dark:
the flame is Imagination's flame
that burns your spirit.
                        When you
are present, but
not present,
                        when you
scarcely sink into sleep
but merely rest in the deadman's float
among waves that never for a moment

133

let up their jostling,
                where you are
                is with the envisioning fire
inside the cave of the mind
where Images ride to the hunt on the creviced walls
as the flame struggles out of the smoke.
All about you is watery, within you lies the dark
cave, and the fire.

. . . .

When you love me well
            it is when
            Imagination has flicked

                            its fire-tongue over you,
                            you are freed
            by that act of the mind
                            to act.
You have
those moments of absolute sureness,
exploding, golden, in the shifting, smoky, uncertain
                            dimensions of the cave,
when the hunter's
                quarry is under his hand,
                breathing, trembling, its heart
racing, and he puts his mark on it,
letting it go until it returns of its own
accord;
            those instants
when the Creative Spirit, sisterly,
takes a Wanderer's cold and burning hand
in hers
and they enter the dance.

Magic

for Jon

The brass or bronze cup, stroked at the rim,
round and around, begins
to hum,
      the hum slowly
buzzes more loudly, and rapidly now
becomes
        the clang of the bell of the
        deep world, unshaken, sounding
        crescendo out of its wide mouth
                one note,
      continuous,
           gong
      of the universe, neither beginning nor ending,
but heard
only those times we take
the cup and stroke
the rim,
diminuendo,
only seeming
to cease when we cease
to listen . . .

135